KATY
STEDING

KATY STEDING

Pro Basketball Pioneer

Sara Gogol

 Lerner Publications Company • Minneapolis

This book is available in two editions:
Library binding by Lerner Publications Company
Soft cover by First Avenue Editions
241 First Avenue North, Minneapolis, Minnesota 55401

Website address: www.lernerbooks.com

Library of Congress Cataloging-in-Publication Data

Gogol, Sara.
    Katy Steding : pro basketball pioneer / Sara Gogol.
      p.   cm.
    Includes bibliographical references (p.) and index.
    Summary: A biography of the young woman who played at Stanford University and on the 1996 Olympic gold–medal basketball team and is now a member of the Portland Power women's professional basketball team.
    ISBN 0–8225–3668–4 (hardcover : alk. paper). — ISBN 0–8225–9823–X (pbk. : alk. paper)
    1. Steding, Katy, 1967– —Juvenile literature. 2. Women basketball players—United States—Biography—Juvenile literature.
    [1. Steding, Katy, 1967– 2. Women basketball players.
3. Basketball players. 4. Women—Biography.] I. Title.
GV884.S75G64   1998
796.323'092—dc21
  [B]   97–53297

Manufactured in the United States of America
1 2 3 4 5 6 – JR – 03 02 01 00 99 98

Contents

After playing all over the world, Katy returned to Portland
to play for her hometown team, the Portland Power.

6

1
Opening Night

Long before game time, fans crowded into the basketball arena. They jostled each other as they bought snacks and souvenirs. They shared a feeling of excitement. Close to 9,000 fans had come to see history being made.

When just a few minutes remained before the opening tip-off, the lights in the arena were dimmed. Spotlights shone on the basketball court. As the home team players were introduced, fans clapped and shouted. Fireworks exploded. Then the crowd noise grew even louder. Katy Steding ran out to the center of the court.

Katy—an Olympic champion—was back home. Katy is a friendly person who isn't conceited. She didn't always believe in how good an athlete she would become. Katy had been a high school basketball star in Oregon. She went on to become a key player on the

Stanford University team. Stanford had won the national championship Katy's senior year. Katy was on the 1996 U.S. Olympic team that won a gold medal. After all that, Katy was back home in Oregon to play professional women's basketball in a brand-new league.

Katy wasn't the only one who had made a journey. Women's basketball has undergone many changes since basketball was invented in 1891. Two eastern women's colleges, Vassar and Smith, had added basketball as a sport in 1892, but many people viewed basketball as too tough for women. These people thought women would get hurt playing a physical sport. They created special rules for girls and women to use when they played basketball. The rules made the game easier. For example, girls and women weren't allowed to run up and down the whole court.

But slowly, people learned that girls and women were capable of playing active sports without any injury. School sports began to change in a big way in 1972 when a law called Title IX was passed. That year, the federal government began to make schools offer girls and women the same opportunities to play sports that boys and men had. In the 1970s, only 7 percent of high school athletes were girls. Twenty years later, 35 percent of high school athletes were girls.

College women's basketball has also grown tremendously. Women's college basketball games are shown on television and often draw big crowds.

These women were Smith College's first basketball team.

For years, the top women players had to go overseas if they wanted to play basketball after college. There was no professional league for them in the United States, so they couldn't play for American fans. But Katy helped to change that. Katy was one of the founding players of the American Basketball League (ABL). When the ABL began, it was the first women's professional basketball league in the United States for many years.

In Portland, Oregon, the large crowd was ready for the ABL's first game to begin. Katy took her position on the court along with the four other starters for her team, the Portland Power. At 6 feet tall, Katy has a slender but strong build. Her job as a **small forward** is to do it all—**rebound,** defend, make passes to open teammates, and shoot. That night, surely everyone in the stands noticed something different about Katy. Her nose was taped up. She had broken it less than a week before in a practice game. Katy wouldn't let a broken nose keep her away from the opening game.

The action was fast and furious. Both teams played hard. Players dove for loose balls, pulled up for **jump shots,** ran plays, faked out defenders, and raced up and down the court.

A group of girls from the Katy Steding Basketball Academy joined in the cheers. The girls had taped up their noses to look like Katy's. Katy may have looked injured, but she played without thinking about her nose. At least until midway through the second quarter, when she was hit hard in the face with the ball.

Katy bent over in pain, covering her face with both hands. Play stopped. Her coach called a timeout. Tears running down her face, Katy left the game and sat down on the bench. Many onlookers wondered if she would be able to return.

Katy's fans supported her, even when she was injured.

With her no-look passes, Katy fires up her team's offense.

Katy considered not going back in. But while she sat on the bench, she gave herself a pep talk. "This is your only home opener," she told herself. "You might as well make the most of it."

Katy went back on the floor and shook off the pain. She got back into a groove and hit a **three-pointer.** In the third quarter, Katy brought down a rebound and rifled a **no-look pass** to a teammate, who made a **lay-up.** Soon afterward, Katy caught a pass and made a reverse lay-up, a difficult shot where a player has to shoot the ball backward over her head.

The large crowd cheered for all of the Portland players' moves. "It just seemed like the roof was going to lift off," Katy remembers. "It was so loud out there." When the game ended, the Portland Power had won. Katy led her team with 16 points and seven **assists.**

Broken nose and all, Katy was playing the game she loved. She was back playing basketball for her hometown fans. And she was playing with and against some of the best players in the world.

Shooting hoops has always been Katy's favorite activity.

2

A Natural

First impressions aren't always right. When Katy was very young, her family couldn't have guessed how far she would go with sports. Katy was born on December 11, 1967 in Portland, Oregon. As a young child, she didn't seem especially athletic, especially compared to her sister Julie, who was three and a half years older.

When Katy was five, her family moved to Lake Oswego, a suburb of Portland. Not long after they moved, Katy's mother and father separated and then divorced. Katy and her sister stayed with their mother and grandmother in their house in Lake Oswego. The girls spent every other weekend with their father, who lived nearby.

Katy was an active girl who liked to be outside. She played baseball, softball, and other games with neighborhood children. She was a catcher in a softball league.

As a child, Katy was artistic as well as athletic.

Katy's interest in basketball started early. When she was in the third grade, she told her mother she wanted to join a basketball league. There was one problem, though. "I want to play," Katy told her mother, "but it's all boys."

Katy's mother suggested that Katy ask a couple of other girls if they wanted to play basketball, too. Katy and two of her friends joined the Youth Basketball

Association (YBA) league. Katy was the only girl on her team, but she wasn't the smallest player. "She was a head taller than everyone on her first team," her mother recalls.

Katy struggled to get used to the league's style of play. At first, she was too timid. She didn't want to hurt anyone's feelings. When her team lost its first game, Katy went home and cried. The boys were "so mean," she told her mother. They kept grabbing the ball out of her hands.

Katy's mom encouraged her. She drove Katy to evening practices during the week and got up early on Saturday mornings to take Katy to games. Katy's mother never said basketball was too rough for girls.

Katy is the girl on the right in the second row in this photograph of her YMCA team.

Katy's father put up a basketball hoop on the garage of her house. Katy and her sister had a good time playing basketball with their dad. Katy remembers making "crazy shots like off the stairs or hanging halfway out of the garage."

It rains a lot in western Oregon, where Katy grew up, but she didn't let that stop her from practicing on her driveway. "I'd go out there in terrible weather," she says, "just to be outside shooting."

"I'd shoot with gloves on so my fingers wouldn't get all soggy and cold," Katy adds. Katy's mother would tell Katy to put on her winter coat, but a bulky parka interfered with Katy's shooting so she would take it off. Her mother often would come out and tell Katy to put her coat back on.

Katy was inspired by Portland's National Basketball Association team, the Trailblazers, which won the NBA championship in 1977. Sometimes while Katy shot hoops by herself, she pretended that she was a player on the championship Trailblazers. When Katy was in fifth grade, she told her classmates that her goal was to become a professional basketball player.

At home, Katy's sister was a strong influence on her. Katy remembers that she and Julie fought "like cats and dogs" when they were growing up. But Katy also looked up to her older sister and admired her achievements in volleyball and basketball. "If Julie can do it, I can do it," Katy told herself.

Julie, Katy's older sister, was an excellent athlete too.

Sports weren't Katy's only interest. She liked to draw, and she always read a lot. At night in bed, after the lights were out, she would read under the covers with a flashlight. Katy also took flute lessons and played in her school band.

But more and more, basketball became the center of Katy's life. In junior high school, she joined her school's basketball team. In high school, she went out for basketball again. By this time she was already 5 feet 11 inches tall. Sometimes being so tall made Katy feel awkward. But playing basketball was something that made Katy feel good about herself.

Gary Lavender was Katy's basketball coach at Lake Oswego High School. He remembers that in Katy's freshman year, "She used to hide from me on the bench in a game." Katy didn't want to take a senior's place on the court.

But Katy couldn't hide her basketball skills. All the hours she'd spent shooting baskets in her driveway had given her deadeye aim as a shooter. "She may be the best pure shooter I've ever seen," Katy's coach told a reporter. And Katy always wanted to improve her game. In high school, she would get the key to the gym from her coach, whom she called "Lav," and would practice shooting by herself.

In the middle of Katy's freshman year, she did become a starter. After that, she started every single game all the way through high school. She played **center** on her team, using her size and strength to rebound, block shots, and score. She set records at her school for scoring and rebounding, and named to the All-State First Team her sophomore, junior, and senior years.

In spite of her high school sports achievements— Katy played four years of varsity volleyball as well as basketball—she didn't let all the attention go to her head. When she got a letter from Stanford University her sophomore year, she showed it to her coach. "Am I good enough?" she asked him.

"You can go anyplace you want, Katy. You've got that much talent," her coach responded.

Coach Lavender was right. Katy received letters from colleges all over the country. In the summer between Katy's junior and senior seasons, Tara VanDerveer, the new women's basketball coach at Stanford University, telephoned Katy. "This is so cool," Katy remembers thinking. Stanford University paid for Katy to tour the campus.

Although basketball became her main love, Katy also played volleyball while she was in high school.

Katy led her team to the state tournament semifinals during her senior season at Lake Oswego High School.

Katy liked the campus, the basketball program, and the solid academic reputation Stanford had. Another plus was that Stanford was in California. That wasn't too far from Oregon. Katy's parents could come see her play. Early in Katy's senior year, she signed a **letter of intent** to play basketball at Stanford.

Signing early took the pressure off Katy during her senior year in high school. Early in the basketball season, she passed the 1,000-point mark for total points. Later that same year, Katy was named the Oregon Class 3A Girls Basketball Player of the Year.

In the semifinals of the high school state tournament, the Lake Oswego Lakers played St. Mary's Academy. The Lakers led in the first half and then their point guard, whose previously broken wrist still hadn't fully healed, got hit across the hand.

Katy carried the team. She put in 24 points, grabbed 21 rebounds, dished off assists, and blocked shots. "She was just awesome," coach Lavender says.

In spite of Katy's effort, her team lost, 54–48. When the final buzzer sounded, Katy fell to the floor in tears. "Lav, I tried so hard," she told her coach.

Even though her team had lost, Katy had showed what kind of player she was. Win or lose, she had always given her high school team everything she had. Now Katy was moving on to college basketball where she would test herself against other top players. She would see how far her "everything" could take her.

Katy and her mother pose during Katy's senior year.

Playing college basketball was a challenge for Katy.

3
College Star

When Katy was a freshman at Stanford, her coach called her the "garbage collector." That may sound like an insult, but to Katy, it was praise. What Katy was "collecting" were offensive and defensive rebounds. Although she was only a first-year player, Katy topped her team in rebounding.

Katy had started her first two college games on the bench. "Everyone is going to be so much better than me," Katy thought at first.

When a Cardinal forward was injured in a game, Katy took her place. She kept the starting spot in the Cardinal lineup. At 6 feet, Katy wasn't tall enough to play center in college basketball, so her coach played her at **power forward.** Katy didn't have to make much of an adjustment. She was still a post player, someone who plays close to the basket but faces away from it until she turns to shoot.

Playing basketball wasn't all that Katy did at college. She had plenty of schoolwork to do, and she also had time to miss her family. Katy's teammates became another kind of family for her. Katy and the other players saw movies together and went to the library to study.

Katy's college coach, Tara VanDerveer, knew that Katy's high school basketball experience had given her a strong foundation. Coach VanDerveer saw that Katy was a naturally athletic player who could rebound well, shoot well, and run the floor well. Shooting was probably Katy's biggest strength, coach VanDerveer thought, but she also liked the way Katy worked hard at improving her game.

Katy's willingness to learn was tested her sophomore year. That year a bigger, stronger freshman took over Katy's spot at power forward. Coach VanDerveer moved Katy to the small forward spot.

The three-point shot had just been added to the college women's game. Katy was a natural choice for a long-range shooter at the small forward position. "Get outside," coach VanDerveer told Katy. "Start working on your three."

Katy calls her sophomore year her "ugly year." Learning to play a new role on court—to face the basket and take an outside shot—wasn't easy. "I'd done things differently all my life," Katy remembers. "It was a tough adjustment for me."

Katy's jumper from behind the three-point line was her
ticket to success on the Stanford team.

Katy decided that her game had to improve. That summer she stayed at Stanford and went to the gym six days a week, shooting for an hour in the morning and playing more basketball at night. When her team took a trip to China that summer to play in exhibition games, Katy's hard work showed in her shooting.

As Katy improved as a player, her team grew stronger, too. When Katy first came to Stanford, the women's basketball team wasn't ranked among the nation's best teams. At the start of Katy's sophomore year, Stanford was ranked 19th in the nation. In Katy's junior year, the Stanford women were among the final eight teams in the NCAA tournament.

Stanford's opponent in the regional final was Louisiana Tech. On game day, Katy felt "really nervous." She and her teammates were in the big time. "Can I really do this?" she asked herself.

Maybe all the pressure affected Katy and her teammates. Katy played good defense and rebounded well, but she didn't shoot well, and Stanford lost.

That summer, Katy went home to Oregon, but she worked hard on the track, in the weight room, and in pickup games. Her senior year, her last season of college basketball, was coming up. "If I didn't put everything I had into it," Katy told herself, "I was going to regret it for the rest of my life."

Katy's self-confidence as a player had grown during her college years. Her coach's confidence in her had grown, too. "She carries us in a lot of situations," coach VanDerveer said about Katy in her senior year. "She hits the big free throws and the big baskets."

The Stanford women won game after game, ending up with a 30–1 regular-season record. But the biggest challenge of all was yet to come. All season the Stanford players had focused on one goal—winning the NCAA championship.

The NCAA tournament is single elimination. No matter how good a team's season has been, one loss in the tournament sends a team home. Stanford won its first game, and then won its second, defeating Hawaii by a whopping 106–76. The Cardinal kept winning and defeated Arkansas in the NCAA West Regional Championship. Katy scored 17 points in that game.

Winning the regional final sent Stanford on to the Final Four in Knoxville, Tennessee. The top four women's college basketball teams in the country would compete against each other. In Stanford's semifinal game, the Cardinal played the University of Virginia. More than 17,000 fans came to watch! Stanford didn't play its best game overall, but Katy came through for her team. She ended up with 18 points and eight rebounds to help her team to a 75–66 victory.

After the game, Katy and her teammates didn't celebrate in the locker room. They were happy about winning, but all they could think about was winning the next game—the championship against Auburn.

"I remember being very hungry," Katy says about that game, "wanting it real bad." Katy was a senior. This was the last game she would ever play with the 11 other women on her team, who had all become her good friends.

More than 16,000 people attended the final game. CBS televised the game to a national audience. All the spectators saw an exciting, fast-paced basketball game. The Auburn Lady Tigers often used a **full-court press.** They pressured the Stanford players whenever Stanford had the ball. In the first half of the game, Stanford had an 11-point lead. Then Auburn came back and was ahead before Stanford tied the score at 41 by halftime.

"If you don't shoot threes, you're coming out," coach VanDerveer had told Katy before the game. Katy listened to her coach and began the game by swishing a three-pointer. By the end of the game, Katy had made 6 of the 15 three-point shots she took, setting a record for most three-point shots made in a championship.

Stanford had the lead late in the game, but Auburn kept fouling to stop the clock. Katy remembers that the final moments of the game were "the longest 20 seconds in my life. You could actually watch the clock click."

Finally, the clock ran out. The Stanford Cardinal had defeated the Auburn Lady Tigers by a score of 88–81. Stanford had won the NCAA championship!

Katy and her teammates cried and hugged. They took turns cutting down pieces of the net for victory souvenirs. "Think of the best hot fudge sundae you've ever had," Katy says, "and put on a lot of extra hot fudge." That was how sweet it felt to win the championship.

But that moment had a bittersweet side to it as well. There would be no more college basketball games for Katy. When she graduated from Stanford with a degree in psychology, she also graduated from the Stanford women's basketball team. What was she going to do next?

Stanford teammate Sonja Henning hugs Katy after a Cardinal victory in the NCAA tournament.

Katy went to Japan to play pro basketball.

4

Basketball Overseas

Katy got lucky. Opportunities to play basketball overseas were opening up for women. Katy didn't have to give up the sport she loved. The Bank of Tokyo offered Katy a job playing basketball in Japan. Her new team was called the Golden Eagles.

At first, Katy was homesick. She felt far away from family and friends, and Japan felt very foreign to her. There was one other American on Katy's team, but her coach and all the other players were Japanese.

Little by little, Katy began to feel more at home in Japan. In her free time, she took lessons in Japanese. She and her Japanese teammates did things together like shopping or cooking American and Japanese dinners for each other.

But just as Katy was starting to feel comfortable in her new country, she injured herself in a game while going up for a lay-up. She didn't push off the way she usually did, and she twisted her leg. She tore the **anterior cruciate ligament** in her right knee. The painful and serious injury would require surgery.

Katy went back to Stanford for the operation. Following the surgery, Katy began her long, demanding rehabilitation on crutches. Then she began running and lifting weights. Getting back into playing shape was tough, but Katy was determined to return to her team in Tokyo and she did the next year.

During the next two seasons, Katy starred for the Golden Eagles. She learned more about Japanese culture and got pretty good at speaking Japanese. One Christmas, Katy's mom and stepfather came to Japan.

Katy and her mother and stepfather visit Mount Fuji.

Katy's Japanese teammates treat her visitors to a feast.

Katy's teammates had a party for Katy and her family. They cooked traditional Japanese food. Everyone sat on the floor and ate in the Japanese style.

In July of 1991, Katy joined the U.S. national team for the World University Games in Sheffield, England. She made an impressive 56 percent of her three-point shots as the U.S. team won the gold. Then Katy went back to her Japanese team.

In 1992, Katy tried out for the U.S. Olympic team. She was one of the last two players cut, along with her former Stanford teammate, Jennifer Azzi. Katy cried when she called her mother to tell her the bad news. But Katy wasn't the sort of person to let a setback get her down for long. She went back to the Golden Eagles.

Katy was getting used to playing in Japan, and she might have stayed there for a number of years. But after her third season there, Japan banned foreign players. Once more, Katy feared her basketball career was over.

Again, she got lucky. A team in Madrid, Spain, hired her. Katy wanted to play basketball, but she never really felt at home in Madrid. She enjoyed traveling in Spain and other European countries, but she was still homesick.

Katy's tough time soon got even tougher. Once again, she tore an anterior cruciate ligament, this time in her left knee. Being injured a second time hit Katy hard. She thought about giving up the sport she loved.

Katy called her mother from Spain but couldn't reach her right away. She telephoned a good friend. Then she spoke with her former coach, Tara VanDerveer.

Coach VanDerveer had told Katy before that she was one of the best shooters around. "Just remember that we need you," the coach said. Coach VanDerveer was the head coach of the next U.S. Olympic team.

In 1992, Katy worked hard to make the U.S. Olympic team, but she was dropped with the final cut.

She wanted Katy on that team, which would play in 1996. Coach VanDerveer raised Katy's spirits. "It's awful right now," the coach said, "but it'll be OK."

Talking to her old coach was exactly what Katy needed. She went to Oregon to have the surgery on her knee. Once again, she rehabilitated an injured knee. But while she was doing that, she did something different as well.

As a college student, Katy had often worked in basketball camps during the summers. After her first knee surgery, she'd helped her former high school coach, Gary Lavender, with his girls basketball team. Teaching young people about basketball wasn't new for Katy. But being a team's coach was.

Katy became the coach for the freshmen boys team at Lake Oswego High School. She was the only woman coaching a boys basketball team in Oregon, and only one other woman in Oregon had ever coached boys high school basketball.

As coach of Lake Oswego High's freshmen boys team, Katy found out that coaching can be frustrating too.

"I really enjoyed working with them," Katy said about the boys, and most people thought that she was a good coach. Still, her focus was more on playing than on coaching. She was aiming for the 1996 Olympic team.

In 1992, the U.S. women's Olympic basketball team had won a bronze medal. The players had trained for a short time together but competed against teams that had been together much longer. After the 1992 Games, USA Basketball and a group of businesses provided enough money so that the U.S. team could train together for more than a year before the 1996 Olympics. Katy wanted to be on that team.

She knew she had to be in top shape for the try-outs. In January 1995, she started training five or six hours a day. She ran on a track, both long distances and short sprints. She spent time in the weight room. She played basketball for a couple of hours every day.

In May 1995, Katy went to Colorado Springs, along with 24 other players. Katy did her best during a long week filled with basketball. When the tryouts were over, she received good news. She was a member of the U.S. National Team. Jennifer Azzi had made the team, too.

Katy and the other women on the U.S. National Team faced some tough challenges. Could this team win the Olympic gold medal for the United States? And could they win over fans for women's basketball?

Katy hustles during Olympic team practices.

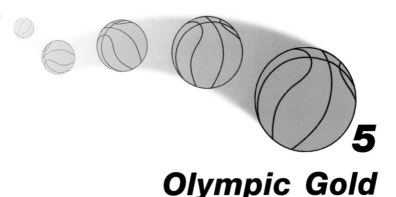

5

Olympic Gold

The clock at the U.S. Olympic Training Center in Colorado Springs didn't show the hour or minutes. That clock kept track of how many days there were until the 1996 Olympics in Atlanta. When Katy and the other players had arrived for the tryouts, the clock showed more than 400 days until the Games would begin.

More than a year may seem like a long time to get ready, but Katy and her teammates had plenty to do. They practiced four hours each day, usually six days a week. They lifted weights, trained on stair machines, and rode stationary bicycles.

They also traveled—a lot. In a little more than a year, the U.S. National Team traveled more than 100,000 miles! "You can wake up and not know what city you're in," Katy told a reporter at one stop.

First, the team went to Italy and Lithuania. Then

the players had the summer off, although they worked out on their own. In late September, the team returned to Colorado Springs and trained for a month there. Katy remembers the two-mile outdoor test that the women ran. The wind was very strong that day, and the temperature was 30 degrees. As Katy came around one corner of the track, she felt as if the wind was grabbing her shirt and holding her back.

Nothing could hold back Katy and her teammates for long, though. They took off on an ambitious tour to play college teams. In two months, the U.S. National Team went to 20 cities—a different city every three days. Katy and her teammates played games against Stanford, Tennessee, Auburn, and the University of Connecticut. Between games, they spoke at grade schools, hospitals, and orphanages. They ended their tour at the University of Colorado, where the U.S. National Team won by an amazing score of 107–24. Katy led her team with 22 points.

In January, the team went to Russia and Ukraine. The first stop was Siberia, which is very cold in the winter. The high temperatures there were around zero! Even at games, the players were so chilly they wore parkas and gloves when they sat on the bench.

Katy was anything but cold on the court. Her primary role was to shoot three-point baskets. Coach VanDerveer called Katy a "zone buster" because she could break down an opposing team's **zone defense** by shooting from the outside. In one game against the Russian team, Katy made five three-point baskets, almost as many as she had made when Stanford won the NCAA championship.

In March, the U.S. team went to China to play the Chinese National Team, which included a player who was 6 feet 8 inches. After the U.S. team defeated China, the U.S. players returned to the United States. They went to the NBA All-Star Game weekend events, in which Katy beat two former NBA stars in a three-point shooting contest. Then in May, the team was back on the road, this time to Australia.

Katy and her teammates were close on and off the court. They went shopping and to movies together. "We had great chemistry," said Katy, who liked every single teammate.

After Jennifer Azzi broke her nose in a game against Cuba, Katy and another girlfriend bought Jennifer a mechanical pig with a wiggling snout. The pig resembled the talking pig in *Babe,* which was one of Jennifer's favorite movies. Soon all the players called the pig "Babe." Babe became their mascot and traveled with them all the way to the Olympics.

All the way was a long way. The U.S. women played 52 games to get ready for the Olympics. They didn't lose a single one! But they were about to face their greatest test. People all over the world would soon be watching them play.

All the U.S. women shared the same dream—an Olympic gold medal. Making this dream come true wouldn't be easy. Their opponents from other countries were strong, fast, and highly skilled.

The U.S. team played Cuba in its opening game. Katy was nervous and excited. "Wow, we're really here," Katy thought as the national anthem played.

Six and a half minutes into the game, Cuba led, 20–13. Then Katy came off the bench. She'd been in the game for just 18 seconds when she caught a pass and made a lay-up. Then Katy stole the ball from a Cuban player. With the score tied at 20, Katy hit a three-pointer to give her team the lead.

The U.S. team defeated the Cubans 101–84. In the first half alone, Katy had 11 points, five rebounds, and one steal.

As the Olympics continued, the starters on the team were on the floor more and more. Players who came in off the bench, like Katy and Jennifer Azzi, played less and less. Katy didn't argue with her coach about playing more. Instead, she played her hardest whenever she got into a game.

The U.S. women beat Ukraine, Zaire, Australia, South Korea, and Japan. In the semifinals, the U.S. team played Australia again, winning 93–71. The U.S. team would play Brazil for the gold medal! In the 1994 world championships, Brazil had beaten the United States. The U.S. team wanted revenge.

Hustling on the court, Katy shows her ball-handling skill.

Katy scrambles for a rebound against the Australians.

Katy's mother and stepfather, her father and stepmother, her boyfriend John Jeub, and John's parents sat in the stands for the gold-medal game. They all wore red jerseys with Katy's name and number in white.

Katy sat on the bench for most of the first half. Near the end of the half, she reported to the scorekeeper that she would be going into the game when the clock stopped for a foul or timeout. Then Katy waited, sitting on a cube close to the scorer's table. But the game clock didn't stop. No fouls were called. No timeouts were called. Katy never got a chance to play.

The Katy Steding cheering section at the Olympics included, from left, her stepmother and father, John Jeub's mother and father, and Katy's mother and stepfather.

Katy wondered if she would have an opportunity to play in the championship game. In the second half, Katy cheered for her teammates from the bench as the U.S. team pulled away from Brazil. Then, coach VanDerveer told Katy to go in. Katy played the last 5 minutes and 11 seconds of the game. She made the one shot she took, a reverse lay-up.

The U.S. team crushed Brazil, winning the gold medal with a 111–87 victory. After the game, Katy and her teammates hugged, cried, and did cartwheels across the arena floor. At the medal ceremony, all 12 of the U.S. players linked arms as they stood together on the podium.

As the national anthem played, Katy felt very proud. "That was the culmination of everything," she remembers. All the long hours of practice, all the traveling, all the games. "It was all worth it."

Katy had her Olympic gold medal. She'd realized her Olympic dream. And that moment of glory would help her move forward toward another dream.

The U.S. women's basketball team celebrates a gold-medal performance at the 1996 Olympic Games. From left, Jennifer Azzi, Lisa Leslie, Carla McGhee, Katy, and Sheryl Swoopes.

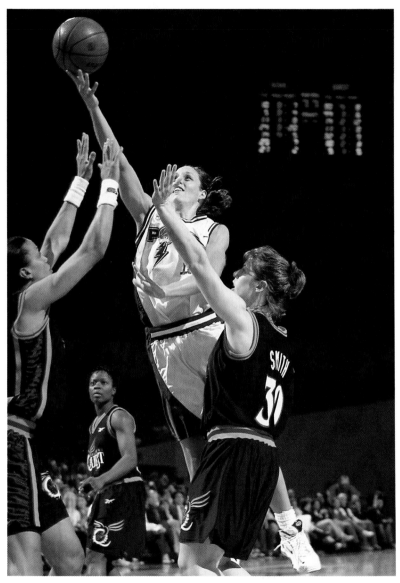

Katy launched her pro career back home in Portland.

Pro Basketball Pioneer

Katy was dreaming big. What she and many others wanted was a women's professional basketball league in the United States.

Some people doubted whether women's professional basketball could succeed in the United States. In the past, leagues had tried and failed. One recent women's pro league had lasted only three years, from late 1978 to early 1981. Other people thought the time was right to try another league because many people had watched the U.S. women's team in the 1996 Summer Olympics. The fans had been impressed by the play of the U.S. women and wanted to see them play more.

Katy and other members of the U.S. national team met to discuss the new league, the American Basketball League (ABL). They talked about how big the court would be, and many other issues. How long a shot clock would the league have? What size ball should the players use?

Katy signed a contract with the ABL, and so did many of her Olympic teammates. Other players joined another new league, the Women's National Basketball Association (WNBA). The ABL played its first season in the fall and winter of 1996-97. The WNBA played its first games the following summer.

Katy and her teammates were turning women's pro basketball into a reality. Achieving a dream isn't easy, though. Katy's first year of pro basketball was a tough one. She had worked with the U.S. national team for more than a year. She didn't even take a break before practice started with her new team, the Portland Power, in September 1996.

Katy loved playing for her hometown fans in Portland, Oregon. She loved being close to her family and friends. Playing basketball in Portland did put some extra pressure on Katy, though. As the hometown heroine and an Olympic medalist, some people expected Katy to be the "star" of her team.

Katy is an excellent shooter and one of the best three-point shooters in the league. More than that, however, Katy is a team player. She never wanted to take most of her team's shots. She would rather make a sharp pass to a teammate closer to the basket. Then, if the teammate was heavily guarded, Katy would catch a pass and shoot.

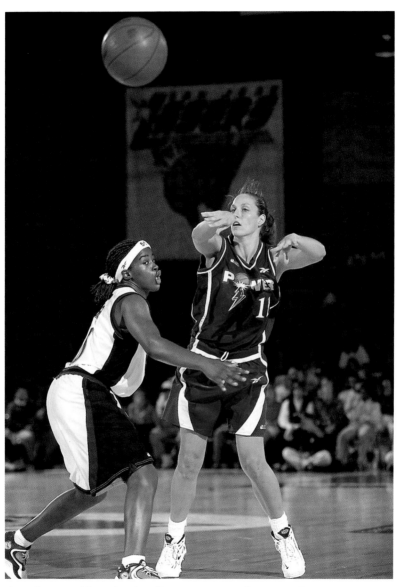

As always, Katy looks first to pass, then to shoot.

A non-stop schedule left Katy dragging after her first year as a professional basketball player.

During Katy's first year of pro basketball, she was tired. It showed in her play. Katy and her teammates played several games a week, traveling to many away games. Everyone got tired, but members of the 1996 Olympic team were especially worn down. By the time the first ABL season ended, Katy had been playing for nearly two years with almost no breaks.

Katy's coach, Lin Dunn, saw Katy become frustrated with herself as a player. Her coach decided to bring Katy in off the bench instead of starting her. Some people thought that not being a starter would make Katy angry. But Katy accepted her coach's decision. Win or lose, bench player or starter, Katy always played as hard as she could.

After the first ABL season, Katy and John Jeub were married. They had postponed their wedding twice, first for the Olympics and then for the first

John and Katy celebrate at their wedding.

ABL season. Some of Katy's teammates came to her wedding. That summer, Katy taught basketball at her own camp. She worked with girls of different ages, teaching them basketball skills. After all, Katy and other women were carving out a basketball future for those girls.

Then in September 1997, Katy started training camp for her second ABL season. She wasn't tired this time. When the regular season started in mid-October, Katy had won back her position as a starter.

The Portland Power played the Seattle Reign in the opening game. Katy's ankle was taped because she'd sprained it about a week earlier. Still, she felt good out on the court. Her ankle didn't bother her. She enjoyed the cheers of the crowd.

Katy and her teammates began to take control of the game in the second quarter. Katy caught a pass, dribbled in toward the basket, then aimed a mid-range jump shot that bounced off the backboard and through the hoop. Her shot tied the game. Then she swished through another to give the Power the lead.

Even when Katy wasn't scoring, she helped her team. She leapt for rebounds, waved her arms on defense, and stuck close to opposing players. She hit the floor to fight for a ball and stole the ball five times. Katy's team won the game by 20 points. Katy had helped with 11 points and four rebounds, plus heads-up play throughout the game.

Katy instructs a young camper at the Katy Steding
Basketball Academy. Katy wants to pass on her skills.

As the game ended, Katy hugged a teammate. She and the other Power players formed a huddle in the center of the court. Together, they raised their hands to signal their victory. The fans were on their feet, clapping and cheering.

Katy's hot play continued. Later in the season, Katy was recovering from another ankle sprain when the Portland Power faced the Atlanta Glory. The score was tied with 19 seconds left in the game. Then Katy grabbed the ball. Dribbling behind the three-point arc, she aimed and launched a shot. The ball rose into the air and dropped through for the game-winning points.

Katy and the Power had a great 1997–98 season. They made it all the way to the ABL semifinals before losing to Long Beach.

Katy loves to compete at this high level. She also knows how important the women's pro game is to many people. Top women players can stay in the United States after college and play for U.S. fans. Girls and boys have top women basketball players to watch, as well as men.

Out on the basketball court, Katy runs the floor, plays in-your-face defense, and swishes her trademark three-point shots. As she plays the sport she loves, she is playing for the future, too. "We're starting something that's going to last," she says. "Twenty years from now, I'll be able to look back and say, 'I was a part of that.'"

Career Highlights

Stanford University

Season	Games	Field Goals			Free Throws			Points	Points per Game	Rebounds	Rebounds per Game
		Made	Attempted	%	Made	Attempted	%				
1986-87	28	118	275	42.9	74	91	81.3	310	11.1	243	8.7
1987-88	32	121	301	40.2	21	63	78.9	319	10.0	221	6.9
1988-89	31	172	377	45.6	66	91	72.5	459	14.8	178	5.7
1989-90	33	180	385	46.8	67	82	81.7	498	15.1	222	6.7
Totals	124	591	1,338	44.2	263	335	78.5	1,586	12.8	864	7.0

1996 Olympic Games

Season	Games	Field Goals			Free Throws			Points	Points per Game	Rebounds	Rebounds per Game
		Made	Attempted	%	Made	Attempted	%				
1996	8	10	25	40.0	3	8	37.5	25	3.1	19	2.4

Portland Power

Season	Games	Field Goals			Free Throws			Points	Points per Game	Rebounds	Rebounds per Game
		Made	Attempted	%	Made	Attempted	%				
1996-97	40	112	284	39.4	87	113	77.0	334	8.4	175	4.4
1997-98	39	112	300	37.3	59	75	78.7	329	8.4	137	3.5
Totals	79	224	584	38.4	146	188	77.7	663	8.4	312	3.9

Glossary

anterior cruciate ligament: A ligament in the center of a person's knee that keeps the leg from extending too far in any direction.

assists: Passes that lead directly to points.

center: A position at which the player, often someone who is tall, plays near the basket.

full-court press: A style of defense in which the defending team closely guards the player with the ball and players likely to receive passes the entire length of the court.

jump shots: Shots in which the shooter jumps and releases the ball at the peak of his or her jump.

lay-up: A shot in which the shooter dribbles toward the basket, pushes off from one leg, and gently bounces the ball off the backboard and into the basket.

letter of intent: A letter in which a high school student-athlete says which college he or she plans to attend.

no-look pass: A pass in which the passer doesn't look at the person to whom he or she is passing.

power forward: A position at which the player plays close to the basket, but not as close as the center. A power forward has many of the same skills and duties as a center but is often shorter than the center.

rebound: To gain control of the ball after a missed shot. An offensive rebound is a rebound by the shooting team. A defensive rebound is a rebound by the defending team.

small forward: A position at which the player plays close to the basket, but not as close as the center or power forward. This player often must shoot from outside and dribble the ball.

three-pointer: A shot that is taken from outside the three-point line on the court. In women's basketball, the three-point line is an arc 19 feet 19 inches from the basket.

zone defense: A style of defense in which each player is assigned to defend a specific area, or zone, of the court.

Sources

Information for this book was obtained from the author's interviews with Katy Steding, Patti Huntley, Gary Lavender, Tara VanDerveer, and Lin Dunn, and the following sources: David Austin (*The Oregonian*, 7 January 1987); Paul Buker (*The Oregonian*, 5 April 1990); Dan Fleser (*The Knoxville News-Sentinel*, 2 April 1990); Ken Goe (*The Oregonian*, 1 January 1990); Hank Hersch (*Sports Illustrated*, 9 April 1990); Dwight Jaynes (*The Oregonian*, 10 February 1996); John Nolen (*The Oregonian*, 26 February 1996); The Portland Power; Jason Quick (*The Oregonian*, 9 December 1996); Mark Rogowsky (*The Stanford Daily*, 2 March 1990); Ed Stackler (*The Stanford Daily*, 19 February 1987); and USA Basketball.

Index

Write to Katy:

You can send mail to Katy at the address on the right. If you write a letter, don't get your hopes up too high. Katy and other athletes get lots of letters every day, and they aren't always able to answer them all.

Katy Steding
c/o The Portland Power
439 North Broadway
Portland, OR 97227

Acknowledgments

Photographs are reproduced with the permission of: © ALLSPORT USA/Stu Forster, p. 1; John Todd/ABL Photos, pp. 2, 6, 12, 53; Smith College Archives, Smith College, p. 9; Alan Spearman/The Oregonian, p. 11; Patti Huntley, pp. 14, 16, 17, 23, 32, 34, 35, 47; Ben Reinbold/Lake Oswego High School, pp. 19, 21; John M. Vincent/The Oregonian, p. 22; © Rod Searcey/Stanford University, pp. 24, 27; AP/Wide World Photos, pp. 31, 49; Tim Defrisco/NBA Photos, pp. 37, 40; Claudia J. Howell/The Oregonian, p. 38; Scott Cunningham/NBA Photos, p. 45; © ALLSPORT USA/Jed Jacobsohn, p. 46; Steve Gibbons/ABL Photos, p. 50; Joel Davis/The Oregonian, pp. 54, 59; Tobin Floom of Images by Floom, Courtesy of Katy Steding, p. 55; © Photo by Linda Kliewer, p. 57.

Front cover photograph by John Todd/ABL Photos.
Back cover photograph by © Linda Kliewer.

Artwork by Steve Schweitzer.

About the Author

Sara Gogol has written three books for young readers, including Lerner's *A Mien Family* and *Vatsana's Lucky New Year*. She also has written a book about women's professional basketball. Sara lives in Portland, Oregon, and teaches English at Portland Community College. She enjoys hiking, bicycling, taking long walks with her dog, and attending women's professional basketball games.